Dr. Tan Kwan Hong

Thailand – In-depth Country Analysis

A Political, Economic and Social Discourse

Anchor Academic
Publishing

Kwan Hong, Tan: Thailand – In-depth Country Analysis. A Political, Economic and
Social Discourse, Hamburg, Anchor Academic Publishing 2016

Buch-ISBN: 978-3-96067-067-4
PDF-eBook-ISBN: 978-3-96067-567-9
Druck/Herstellung: Anchor Academic Publishing, Hamburg, 2016
Covermotiv: © pixabay.de

Bibliografische Information der Deutschen Nationalbibliothek:
Die Deutsche Nationalbibliothek verzeichnet diese Publikation in der Deutschen
Nationalbibliografie; detaillierte bibliografische Daten sind im Internet über
http://dnb.d-nb.de abrufbar.

Bibliographical Information of the German National Library:
The German National Library lists this publication in the German National Bibliography.
Detailed bibliographic data can be found at: http://dnb.d-nb.de

All rights reserved. This publication may not be reproduced, stored in a retrieval system
or transmitted, in any form or by any means, electronic, mechanical, photocopying,
recording or otherwise, without the prior permission of the publishers.

Das Werk einschließlich aller seiner Teile ist urheberrechtlich geschützt. Jede Verwertung
außerhalb der Grenzen des Urheberrechtsgesetzes ist ohne Zustimmung des Verlages
unzulässig und strafbar. Dies gilt insbesondere für Vervielfältigungen, Übersetzungen,
Mikroverfilmungen und die Einspeicherung und Bearbeitung in elektronischen Systemen.

Die Wiedergabe von Gebrauchsnamen, Handelsnamen, Warenbezeichnungen usw. in
diesem Werk berechtigt auch ohne besondere Kennzeichnung nicht zu der Annahme,
dass solche Namen im Sinne der Warenzeichen- und Markenschutz-Gesetzgebung als frei
zu betrachten wären und daher von jedermann benutzt werden dürften.

Die Informationen in diesem Werk wurden mit Sorgfalt erarbeitet. Dennoch können
Fehler nicht vollständig ausgeschlossen werden und die Diplomica Verlag GmbH, die
Autoren oder Übersetzer übernehmen keine juristische Verantwortung oder irgendeine
Haftung für evtl. verbliebene fehlerhafte Angaben und deren Folgen.

Alle Rechte vorbehalten

© Anchor Academic Publishing, Imprint der Diplomica Verlag GmbH
Hermannstal 119k, 22119 Hamburg
http://www.diplomica-verlag.de, Hamburg 2016
Printed in Germany

Table of Contents

Contents	Page
Thailand's Situational Overview	5
How This Report Is Organized	9
Domestic Challenges	
1. The Unsettling Political Climate (Political Challenges)	
a. Overview	11
b. Current Challenges	
i. Political Corruption	12
ii. Poor Governance Indicators	13
c. Future Risks	
i. Increasing Insurgency in the South	14
ii. Political Instability	15
2. Unsustainable Economic Fundamentals (Economic Challenges)	
a. Overview	17
b. Current Challenges	
i. High Inflation and Debt	18
ii. Increasing Fiscal Deficit	19
c. Future Risks	
i. Decline in Loan Growth Rates	20
ii. Flood and Natural Disasters' Impact on Thai Industry	20
3. Tackling the Multi-Faceted Social Ills (Social Challenges)	
a. Overview	23
b. Current Challenges	
i. Regional Disparity	24
ii. Outbreak of Diseases	25

c. Future Risks	
i. Market Distortions due to Wage Hikes	26
ii. Rising Unemployment	27
Foreign Policy Challenges	
1. Preah Vihear Temple – The Temple of Dispute	29
a. ICJ and ASEAN's Intervention	31
b. Thailand's Local Politicization the Main Cause of Conflict Escalation	32
c. Conflict Expands Beyond the Temple	32
d. Further Attempts at Conflict Resolution	33
e. A Lose-Lose Situation for Both Countries	33
2. Thailand's Alliance with China versus the US: A Delicate Balance to pleasing both "Masters"	35
a. The Perception of an Existential Threat	35
b. Domestic Political and Economic Interests	37
c. The Challenge of Having Limited Strategic Pre-Dispositions	38
3. Thailand's Indecisiveness with Regionalization	40
Thailand – Facts and Figures	43
Outlook for 2012 – 2016	44
About The Author	45

Thailand's Situational Overview

Stimulating the economic vibrancy of Thailand through enhancing market access for businesses and through trade promotions came up as the primary focus of Prime Minister Yingluck Shinawatra's coalition government. However, widespread corruption plagues the country's political and bureaucratic machinery. Prime Minister Yingluck Shinawatra's amnesty plan for politicians, which may grant her elder brother and former Prime Minister Thaksin Shinawatra to re-enter the country, could exacerbate further political distrust.

The government has also committed to spending THB 600-800 billion (US $19.6-26.2 billion) on rebuilding the country, which could help tackle the ramifications caused by the recent floods. However, the strain imposed on the fiscal budget will further worsen the deficit, making it an uphill task for the government to maintain strong public finances for both social welfare and economic development initiatives.

The Thai government was also committed to improving social protection, encapsulated via the 11th Economic and Social Development Plan. Prime Minister Yingluck Shinawatra aims to provide solutions to counter the peril of drugs, ward off and eradicate corruption, enhance the living standards of the people through wage increases and tax relief, and improve the health insurance system. Unfortunately, the country suffers from income and development disparity.

Thailand's innovation scenario has shown respectable growth over the past year, with the quantity of patents granted to Thailand by the US Patent and Trademark Office (USPTO) growing from 25 in 2005 to 60 in 2010. The overall research and development (R&D) scenario is making remarkable progress. This positive phenomenal is credited to the regular and unwavering encouragements to innovation by the government. Moving forward, Thailand will need to improve the robustness of its enforcements of intellectual property rights (IPR), and attract an increasing number of engineers and skilled technical personnel so as to cover the current shortage of talent in these areas.

Thailand maintains an independent judicial system, responsible for maintaining law and order within the country. Also, according to the World Bank's Doing Business 2012 report, which measures the ease of doing business within an economy, Thailand ranked an impressive 17th out of 183 economies measured. Thailand has committed itself to massive tax reforms that encourage investments and improve market conditions through domestic expenditure. However, weak labor laws that do not guarantee equal rights and protection for all in the workforce does continue to inhibit the country's progress. Further, there exist government investment regulations that are lacking in compatibility with current market needs.

Thailand has in place a robust environmental strategic framework to counter its energy and environmental concerns. Since October 2010, the government has agreed to impose a new tax scheme of polluting industries as part of its efforts in environmental conservation. However, rapid economic development, increased urbanization and massive industrial expansion have adversely impacted the country's ecosystems. Air pollution is also a worry, as carbon dioxide (CO_2) emissions escalated from 187 million metric tonnes in 2002 to around 268 million metric tonnes in 2010.

On the foreign policy front, ties with Cambodia, despite improving since Yingluck ascended the premiership, still faces risks stemming from both countries' dispute over both the Preah Vihear temple, and on the 4.6 square kilometer area of land adjacent to the temple.

Also, due to a lack of a common existential threat, coupled with the domestic political and economic issues, and the need to maintain close relations with China, Thailand faces severe limitations that prevents it from a full and whole-hearted engagement with the US, reaping only marginal benefits from the overall resources poured into the region by the US in support of its 'pivot' strategy.

Further, how Thailand can develop an effective engagement policy towards recent regional developments over the establishment of the ASEAN Community and the Trans-Pacific Partnership (TPP) remains a concern.

Figure 1: The Map of Thailand

Source: CIA, The World Factbook

How This Report Is Organized

This report is segregated into 2 major segments: Domestic Challenges and Foreign Policy Challenges. A total of 3 major domestic challenges and 3 major foreign policy challenges are highlighted and are all extensively expounded upon.

The 3 domestic challenges highlighted are:

1. The Unsettling Political Climate (Political Challenges)
    a. Overview
    b. Current Challenges
        i. Political Corruption
        ii. Poor Governance Indicators
    c. Future Risks
        i. Increasing Insurgency in the South
        ii. Political Instability
2. Unsustainable Economic Fundamentals (Economic Challenges)
    a. Overview
    b. Current Challenges
        i. High Inflation and Debt
        ii. Increasing Fiscal Deficit
    c. Future Risks
        i. Decline in Loan Growth Rates
        ii. Flood Impact on Industry
3. Tackling the Multi-Faceted Social Ills (Social Challenges)
    a. Overview
    b. Current Challenges
        i. Regional Disparity
        ii. Outbreak of Diseases

      c. Future Risks
   - i. Market Distortions due to Wage Hikes
   - ii. Rising Unemployment

For each of the domestic challenge described above, an overview is written on it, coupled with 2 current challenges and 2 future risks faced in each challenge.

In addition, 3 foreign policy challenges are highlighted and are titled as such:

1. Preah Vihear Temple: The Temple of Dispute
2. Thailand's Alliance with China versus the US: A Delicate Balance to pleasing both "Masters"
3. Thailand's Indecisiveness with Regionalization

A section on Thailand's Major Facts and Figures are also included.

Domestic Challenge 1
The Unsettling Political Climate

Overview

Thailand has been actively encouraging higher levels of public investments in the pursuit of rapid economic progress in the country. The coalition government chaired by Prime Minister Yingluck Shinawatra aims to stimulate economic vibrancy by enhancing market access for businesses and by promoting trade and investments through a more robust set of laws, regulations and investment promotion activities. However, widespread corruption plagues its political and bureaucratic machinery, which constitutes an inhibition to investments.

Thailand's performance in terms of governance indicators remained at best, abysmal. On top of the increasing violence and insurgency in Southern Thailand, the threat of political instability adds on to Thailand's woes. Core to this political instability lays the claim that Yingluck is working on an amnesty for politicians that could pave the way for former Prime Minister Thaksin Shinawatra's return to the country. The impetuous and dubious manner in which the pardon decree has been introduced has raised doubts about the government's intentions. Thaksin's return could yet again sparkle another political turmoil, as the opposition Democrat Party, the military, and the anti-Thaksin defense establishment could all collaborate once more to topple the government.

Figure 2: Analysis of Thailand's Political Landscape

Current Strengths	Current Challenges
• Prudent Macro-economic Policies	• Political Corruption
	• Poor Governance Indicators
Future Prospects	**Future Risks**
• Improving Relations with China	• Increasing Insurgency in the South
	• Political Instability

Note: For the case of this report, only the Current Challenges and Future Risks will be expounded upon.

Current Challenges

Political corruption

Thailand's growth has been stalled with massive levels of corruption. Indeed, extensive corruption in the country's political and bureaucratic machinery has been a serious issue for many years. At the institutional level, it has traditionally hindered prospective investments. According to Transparency International's 2010 Corruption Perceptions Index, which measures perceived levels of public sector corruption, Thailand ranked a dismal 78th out of 178 countries surveyed. Affirming this phenomenal is the World Bank's 2010 Worldwide Governance Indicators, which ranked the country in the 46.9 percentile for control of corruption.

The country also faces a history of scandals. In August 2008, 44 people were involved in the THB1.4billionn (US$42 million) rubber saplings procurement scam during Thaksin Shinawatra's administration. The Supreme Court's Criminal Division for Holders of Political Positions subsequently charged them with alleged corrupted practices.

In 2009, the Customs Department was ranked the highest among all government agencies in terms of the number of complaints filed regarding corruption. Former Prime Minister Abhisit Vejjajiva's government also wasn't free from corruption scandals during their administration. The government's then US$42 million stimulus package to combat recession was beset by procurement scams and corrupted deals due to patronage politics, leading to the resignation of two ministers. Accounting irregularities were discovered in the procurement of hospital equipments and school supplies and the award of construction tenders.

Most ridiculously, the chief of the Bhumjaithai Party, Chavarat Chanvirakul, was alleged to have auctioned provincial governor posts to the highest bidders, as well as indulging himself in real estate deals.

The Thai military, with a budget that has doubled since the 2006 coup, is also known to be a fertile ground for corruption and inflated costs.

Finally, Political parties squabbling over corruption charges could lead to political instability.

Poor governance indicators

Thailand's performance as measured by the World Bank's Worldwide Governance Indicators has been a disappointment. In 2010, in the voice and accountability category, the country was awarded a percentile rank of 30.3, a significant decline from its year 2000 rank of 63.9. In terms of political stability, it ranked in the 12.7 percentile, a low score that resulted from the frequent military coups and government changes. In terms of government effectiveness, it was ranked in the 58.4 percentile, reflecting an administration of public agencies not free from political pressures, as well as the dismal quality of policy formulation and implementation.

Thailand was also ranked in the 56.5 percentile in terms of regulatory quality. This underpins the restrictive regulations on business, labor, and rights to property, on top of its inefficient bureaucratic functions which imposes unnecessary restrictions, further hampering investments.

Finally, in terms of the rule of law and the control of corruption, the country was ranked in the 49.8 and the 46.9 percentiles respectively. Both rankings are below that of Malaysia and Singapore.

Thus, Thailand still has much to improve on when proper and credible governance is concerned. A continued poor performance in these rankings will only inhibit Thailand's growth in the long run.

Future Risks

Increasing insurgency in the south

Insurgency in Southern Thailand is on the rise, and has had devastating consequences. Wars were fought in the jungle-covered provinces of Southern Thailand, which borders Malaysia, and separatists had already killed more than 4,000 people since the conflicts started in 2004. These separatists are also the perpetuators of an increasing number of car bomb explosions, with attacks of this nature rising from just three cases in 2010, to six cases between January and August 2011 alone.

An army with an estimated size of 40,000 Thai soldiers is fending off the insurgency in the south.

Before the commencement of the elections, Yingluck Shinawatra promised the region greater autonomy by combining the three southern provinces of Yala, Pattani and Naratiwat into a single special administrative zone with a single elected governor. However, this proposal wasn't well received by the interior ministry and the military. Prime Minister Yingluck Shinawatra has also appointed a retired general, who was once responsible for the shelling of Southern Thailand's holiest mosque in 2004, for the top national security job. This indicated that the government could stand to take a tough stance against the insurgence. While the government hesitates over a coherent strategy for Southern Thailand, the insurgency is only worsening and claiming more lives.

Political instability

Political instability once again is the bane to Thailand's development. Street demonstrations that were believed to be inspired and instigated by former Prime Minister Thaksin Shinawatra managed to sway the opposition Pheu Thai Party (led by Thanksin's sister Yingluck Shinawatra) to victory in the July 2011 elections. The Yingluck government is reportedly working on amending the Defense Administration Act to allow greater government control over the military. The prime minister is also alleged to be amending an amnesty for politicians that could enable Thaksin's return to the country. New eligibility conditions to the amnesty decree were approved, while the cabinet deleted certain clauses enforced in 2010 that does not grant amnesty for those convicted for drug trafficking and corruption. The impetuous and dubious manner in which the pardon decree has been introduced has raised doubts about the government's intentions. The opposition demands that Thaksin should not be forgiven, having disregarded the Thai justice system by refusing to serve his jail term. To certain political factions, Thaksin's return would definitely be undesirable. For example, the anti-Thaksin establishment, in support of the Democrat Party, could enjoy favorable political fortunes if the military were to exercise another coup to overthrow the ruling government. All these factors will only result in political instability.

Figure 3: Thailand – Key Political Figures

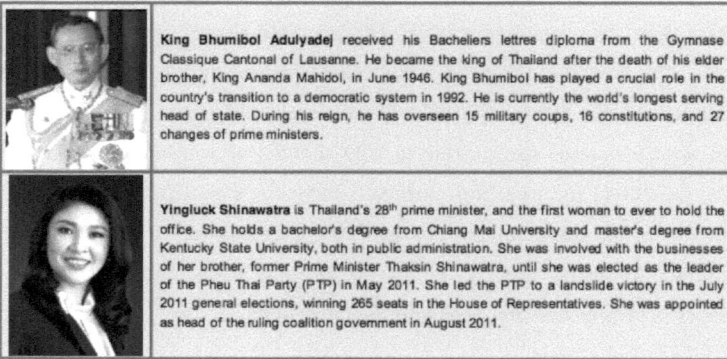

King Bhumibol Adulyadej received his Bacheliers lettres diploma from the Gymnase Classique Cantonal of Lausanne. He became the king of Thailand after the death of his elder brother, King Ananda Mahidol, in June 1946. King Bhumibol has played a crucial role in the country's transition to a democratic system in 1992. He is currently the world's longest serving head of state. During his reign, he has overseen 15 military coups, 16 constitutions, and 27 changes of prime ministers.

Yingluck Shinawatra is Thailand's 28th prime minister, and the first woman to ever to hold the office. She holds a bachelor's degree from Chiang Mai University and master's degree from Kentucky State University, both in public administration. She was involved with the businesses of her brother, former Prime Minister Thaksin Shinawatra, until she was elected as the leader of the Pheu Thai Party (PTP) in May 2011. She led the PTP to a landslide victory in the July 2011 general elections, winning 265 seats in the House of Representatives. She was appointed as head of the ruling coalition government in August 2011.

Source: Datamonitor

Figure 4: Key Political Events Timeline

Pre-1945	1946–90	1991–2001	2002–06	2007 onwards
• In 1917, Siam became the ally of Great Britain in World War I. • In 1932, Peoples Party organized a revolution which compelled King Prajadhipok to abandon absolute monarchy for constitutional monarchy. • In 1939, the country changed its name from Siam to Thailand. • In 1941, Japan and Thailand entered into a ten-year agreement under which Thailand agreed to assist Japan militarily, politically and economically against Britain and the US.	• In 1946, King Ananda was assassinated. • During 1965–75 Thailand permitted the US to use its base during the Vietnam War. • In 1971, the armed forces of Thailand carried out a bloodless coup and suspended the cabinet and declared martial law. • In 1976, the coalition government was overthrown by a military coup. • In 1978, Thanin Kraivichien's government was overthrown by a military coup in Bangkok, and a "Revolutionary Council" of more than 20 high profile officers took control.	• In 1991, Major General Chatichai Choonhaven's leadership collapsed after the armed forces seized power. Anand Panyarachun was named the prime minister. • In 1992, General Suchinda Kraprayoon, hitherto supreme commander of the armed forces, was appointed as the prime minister. However, he was forced to resign. He was replaced by Chuan Leekpai. • In 1996, Chavalit Yongchaiyudh of the New Aspiration Party won the elections. • In 2001, leader of the Thai Rak Thai Party Thaksin Shinawatra won the general elections and formed a coalition government.	• In 2002, the Thai army fired shells into Burma during the battle between Burmese army and ethnic Shan rebels, triggering a diplomatic row. • In the 2005 elections, Thaksin Shinawatra was re-elected by a greater majority, securing more than 350 of the 500 parliamentary seats. • In 2005, with the continuing violent unrest in the south, Mr. Thaksin resorted to counter suspected Muslim militants in the region using a military offensive. • In February 2006, Mr. Thaksin suspended the National Assembly in response to a growing campaign for his resignation.	• Due to post-election turmoil, Mr. Thaksin stepped down, but resumed his post in May 2006. • In 2007, corruption charges were filed against Mr. Thaksin and his wife. • After massive street protests, parliament elected Abhisit Vejjajiva as prime minister on December 15, 2008. • Pro-Thaksin protesters began demonstrations against the government from 2009 up to May 2011, when elections were announced. • In the July 2011 Elections, the Pheu Thai Party won under the leadership of Yingluck Shinawatra, who was elected as prime minister.

Source: Datamonitor

Domestic Challenge 2
Unsustainable Economic Fundamentals

Overview

Thailand is a major international financial hub, supported by an integrated banking system network. Sensible fiscal and monetary policies advanced the country's economy in recent years. A diversified manufacturing sector is a major proponent of growth, and the industrial sector contributed 44.7% of Thailand's overall GDP in 2010.

The government has committed to spending THB 600 TO 800 billion (US$19.6 TO 26.2 billion) on rebuilding the country with the aim of reversing the negative impact caused by the floods.

Also, the country's expanding capital market constitutes a significant driver towards the development of the economy, serving as a source of funds for all business sectors and providing a viable destination for domestic and international investments.

However, a concern lies in the worsening fiscal deficit that will make it an uphill climb for the government to maintain robust public finances in support of both social welfare and economic development initiatives. This budget deficit will rise to around THB400 billion (US$13.4 billion) by 2012, amounting to 3.9% of total GDP. In addition, high inflationary levels and debt will do nothing to assist the country in tackling its weak public finances.

Finally, as estimated by the Thai Chamber of Commerce, the floods that have ravaged the country since 2011 have had a significant impact, costing the economy a loss of US$22 billion on top of 1 million job losses.

Figure 5: Analysis of Thailand's Economic Landscape

Current Strengths	Current Challenges
• Well-Developed Banking System • Strong Manufacturing Sector	• High Inflation and Debt • Increasing Fiscal Deficit
Future Prospects	**Future Risks**
• Flood Reconstruction expenditure • Decreasing Levels of Inflation	• Decline in Loan Growth Rates • Flood Impact on Industry

Note: For the case of this report, only the Current Challenges and Future Risks will be expounded upon.

Current Challenges

High inflation and debt

High inflation has long been the weakness of the Thai economy. The country's inflationary levels severely increased from 0.7% in 2002, to 4.7% over just four years in 2006, hitting 5.5% in 2008. The rising inflation recorded during early 2008 was the result of rising energy and food prices. Although there was a deflation of 0.8% in 2009, economic revival in 2010 pushed inflation up to 3.3%. High commodity prices are expected to create upward inflationary pressures in 2011. With floods devastating the country not too long ago, the prices of essentials are also expected to increase, increasing inflation even further over the middle term.

Thus, high inflation will not be favorable as the country seeks to tackle its weak public finances in recent years.

Figure 6: Consumer price index and consumer price index-based inflation in Thailand, 2004-14

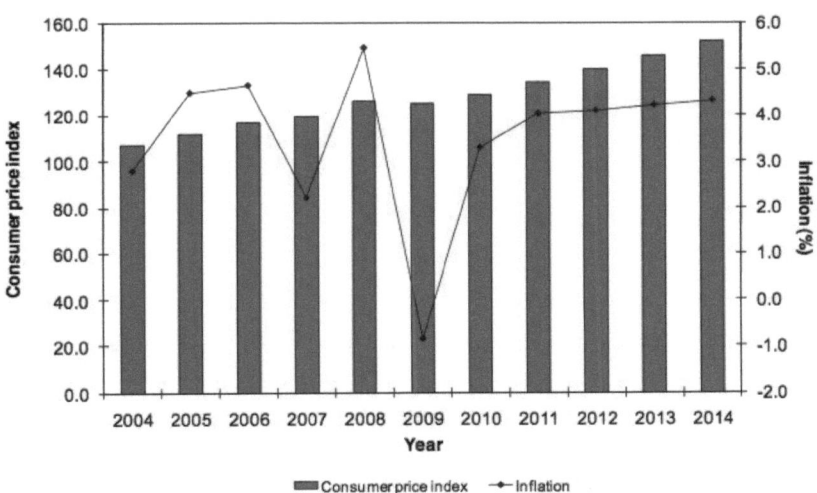

Source: Datamonitor

Increasing fiscal deficit

The government has allocated an increasing national budget, from THB 2.1 trillion (US$63.5 billion) in 2010-11, to THB 2.3 trillion (US$77.2 billion) for the year 2011-12. They have placed greater emphasis on social disparity reduction, a long-lingering issue in Thai society.

In 2012, the government allocated substantial funds on flood recovery and rehabilitation, supported by an expenditure of THB 2.38 trillion (US$77.2 billion). If the populist policies made by the current government during its election campaign were to be implemented, these initiatives could cost a total of THB 2 trillion (US$65.4 billion) over five years.

The budget deficit in 2010 was US$8.1 billion, or 2.7% of the GDP. The increasing fiscal deficit will compromise a strong public finance position, making if difficult for the government to support both social welfare and economic development programs in the future.

Future Risks

Decline in loan growth rates

Due to the devastating impact of the floods on industrial provinces, loan growth generated by the country's premium banks is expected to decline. Many of Thailand's largest banks, such as Kasikornbank, Siam Commercial Bank and Bangkok Bank, the country's largest lender, reported a declining loan growth rate in the forth quarter, despite it generally being the peak quarter for lending. The growth in bank lending is also influenced by economic growth, and the lower GDP growth forecast of subsequent years is expected to generate repercussions for bank lendign growth rates.

Flood and natural disasters' impact on Thai industries

The possibility of future floods remains a certainty. Natural disasters that happen on foreign soil could also cause devastation to Thailand's economic health. Additionally, the ability of the government and the public sector to deal with these potential future floods constitutes a future risk factor that, if not done well, can pose serious difficulties for future Thai economic growth.

2011 has demonstrated a clear case study. In March 2011, many manufacturing companies in Thailand were dependent on imports of components and parts from Japan, and were thus severely affected when the earthquake and tsunami hit Japan in brutal fashion. Companies, especially those operating in the automotive and electronics sectors have been unable to receive shipment of Japanese components.

Figure 7: Japanese Imports Constitutes the Largest Share of Total Imports to Thailand in 2010

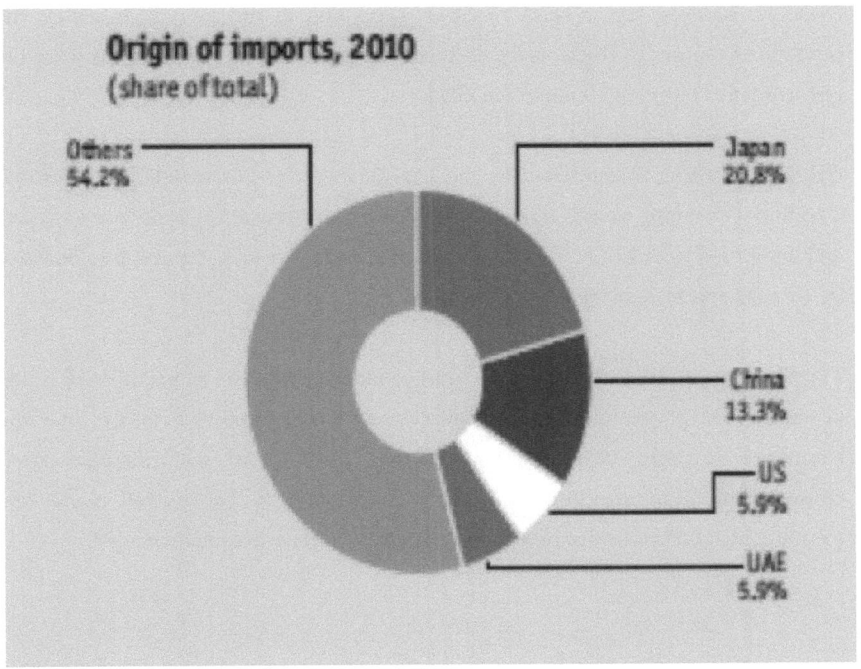

Source: McInnis CIT, EIU, EXIM, Ministry of Commerce

Adding to these woes, the unforgiving floods that have mercilessly ravaged the country since July 2011 have had adverse consequences to numerous Thai industries. These floods have shut down seven industrial estates situated in the north of Bangkok, affecting nearly 10,000 factories and more than 660,000 jobs. This severely compromised the output and earnings of the electronics and automotive sectors. The country's transport infrastructure were shut down and rendered useless, causing major disruptions to the supply chains of the manufacturing sector.

Even the tourism sector wasn't spared. According to the tourism ministry, the number of visitors to the country declined rapidly by up to 1 million, vis-à-vis the government's target of 19 million in 2011.

Overall, according to estimated by the Thai Chamber of Commerce, the estimated cost to the economy caused by the floods due to declining output and loss of assets, had amounted to US$33 billion. 12 million jobs were also loss. Exports also declined in the subsequent year following the floods.

Thus, such exogenous shocks to the Thai economy posses an impactful risk to the economy. The government and the public sector will have to dedicate time and resources towards developing alternative plans that will increase their responsiveness to dealing with such predicaments. Thoughtful plans and meaningful actions taken to reduce or mitigate such risks are much needed.

Domestic Challenge 3
Tackling the Multi-Faceted Social Ills

Overview

The Thai government was also committed to improving social protection, encapsulated via the 11th Economic and Social Development Plan. Prime Minister Yingluck Shinawatra aims to provide solutions to counter the peril of drugs, ward off and eradicate corruption, enhance the living standards of the people through wage increases and tax relieves, and improves the health insurance system. The country boosts a large educated workforce, with a high literacy rate of 95.7% out of the total population in 2010.

However, both income and development disparity are commonplace, and while Bangkok and its suburbs are prospering, the barren northeast faces a different fate, and will continue to remain underdeveloped and poor over the next decade.

In addition, with thousands of homes surrounded by water caused by the floods since 2011, an outbreak of diseases due to the receding floodwaters could be plausible. Future floods that could occur in the future are likely to produce such hazards too.

The government's decision to increase minimum daily wages to a flat rate of THB 300 (US$10) has attracted antagonism from businesses, and its populist measures may result in market distortions that will impact the business friendliness of the country.

The government's move to raise the minimum daily wage to a flat rate of THB300 ($10) has attracted opposition from businesses, and its populist measures may result in market distortions that will impact the business friendliness of the country.

Figure 8: Analysis of Thailand's Economic Landscape

Current Strengths	Current Challenges
• Strong Social Policies • Highly Educated Population	• Regional Disparity • Outbreak of Diseases
Future Prospects	**Future Risks**
• Expansion of Traditional Thai Medicine	• Market Distortions due to Wage Hikes • Rising Unemployment

Note: For the case of this report, only the Current Challenges and Future Risks will be expounded upon.

Current Challenges

Regional disparity

Income and development disparity are typical in a developing country like Thailand. While Bangkok and its suburbs are prospering, the barren northeast faces a different fate, and will continue to remain underdeveloped and poor over the next decade. The rapid economic growth in and around Bangkok has further marginalized the country's less developed regions. And while efforts have been made by previous Thai governments to counter this regional development disparity through provincial programs such as the Eastern Seaboard project and other populist policies, this disparity still remains, and will remain as an obstacle to Thailand's social and economic development.

Furthermore, income inequality remains a significant issue. This stunning inequality of income and wages can be demonstrated by comparing employee earnings in the public and private sectors of different regions. For example, employees in the northeast region receive an average wage that are around three times lower than those in Bangkok and twice as low as those in the central region.

Per capita government expenditure in the northeast, particularly on health and agriculture, are also comparatively lower than in other regions, and lags below that of the central region by almost half.

Finally, tackling this disparity of income and development constitutes an urgent issue for the government. Not doing so quickly and well enough could lead to increased crime rates and anti-national activities in the country.

Outbreak of diseases

The country's medical authorities have issued a warning of a plausible outbreak of diseases due to the receding floodwaters.

As of November 2011 to early 2012, half of Bangkok was still submerged in floodwaters. Several regions of Bangkok were in the course of water flows from the north to the Gulf of Thailand, and the city faces a net inflow of 100 million cubic meters of water every day. With thousands of households encircled by water since July 2011, disease outbreaks thus became a serious problem.

Water contaminated by urine from animals poses a risk of bacterial infection to humans, especially to women. The population also faces the potential threat of cholera, gastrointestinal diseases, and typhoid, while millions of people who were displaced due to the floods are faced with contaminated food, water and an unhygienic environment. This poses a significant obstacle that the country must resolve.

Future Risks

Market distortions due to wage hikes

Policies by the government to raise the minimum daily wage to a flat rate of THB 300 (US$10) have met with resistance from businesses. Before this announcement, the minimum daily wages were made unequal across the provinces, from a high of THB 221 (US$7.20) in Phuket to a low of THB 159 (US$5.20) in the northern province of Phayao.

The government's move to raise the minimum daily wage to a flat rate of THB300 ($10) has attracted opposition from businesses. Prior to the government's announcement, the minimum daily wage varied across the provinces, from a high of THB221 ($7.20) in Phuket to a low of THB159 ($5.20) in the northern province of Phayao.

Businesses were worried that a sudden sharp raise in wage bills without a matching increase in productivity will not financially sustainable.

Further, the government intends to raise the minimum monthly income for upcoming university graduates from THB 10,640 (US$348) to THB 15,000 ($491).

Due to these populist measures, business friendliness and viability will thus be adversely impacted in the country.

Rising unemployment

The Thai manufacturing sector were also adversely impacted by the earthquake and resulting tsunami in Japan. The merciless tsunami, which had devastated entire towns and industrial zones supplying electronic and automotive components needed by the Thai manufacturing sector, also posed far reaching impact on the unemployment issues of Thailand.

Japan is also Thailand's largest import partner.

As an added curse, the floods that have been menacing Thailand since 2011 have also severely impacted the country's manufacturing and tourism sectors, resulting in massive loss of jobs.

From 2001 to 2010, employment grew at an average of 1.4%. In contrast, according to Datamonitor, employment growth rates are expected to decline to an average of 0.6% for the 2011 to 2016 period. The persistent flooding is therefore expected to create an increasing unemployment in the country, leading on to adverse social ills.

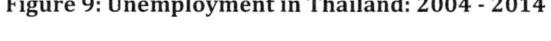

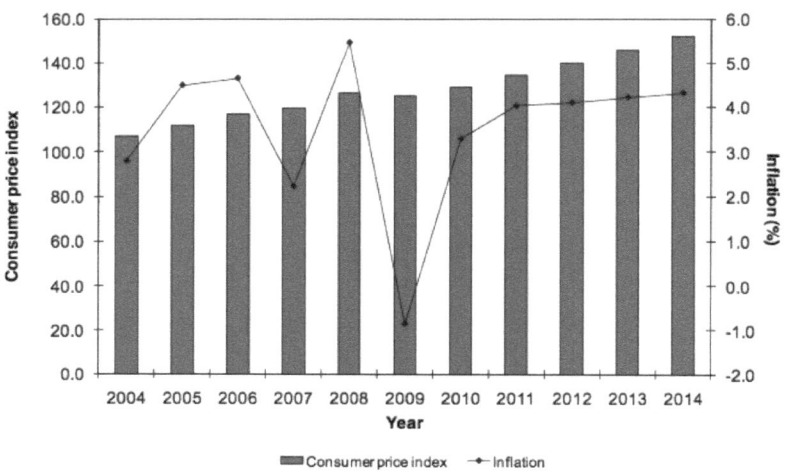

Source: Datamonitor

Foreign Policy Challenge 1
Preah Vihear Temple: The Temple of Dispute

An ancient Hindu temple build during the reign of the Khmer Empire during the ninth-century would unknowingly spark a contentious and unsettling bilateral relationship between Cambodia and Thailand centuries later. Sitting atop a 525-metre cliff in the Dângrêk Mountains, Preah Vihear province in Cambodia, the temple became the source of a lengthy dispute between the two countries since 1962, when both countries contested over its ownership. The case was then referred to the International Court of Justice (ICJ) in The Hague, who then awarded the ownership of the temple in Cambodia's favor.

Decades later till today, despite the ICJ's 1962 ruling supporting Cambodia's ownership, this issue remained far from resolved. In fact, relationships between both countries have gotten so sour that it sparked a standoff around the temple for several years, including several military and armed confrontations during that period.

Figure 10: The Preah Vihear Temple

Source: Asiavipa.com

Figure 11: Location of the Preah Vihear Temple – At the Borders of Thailand and Cambodia

Source: Wikipedia

ICJ and ASEAN's Intervention

Cambodia had repeatedly turned to the ICJ for help. In 2011, Cambodia approached the ICJ once more on issues of Thai encroachment on its claimed territory. This resulted in an ICJ announcement calling for both countries to retract their military presence:

"Both parties must immediately withdraw their military personnel currently present in the provisional demilitarized zone, then refrain from any military presence within that zone and from any armed activity directed at that zone."

ICJ intended for the demilitarized zone to be perceived as a renewed invitation to Thailand and Cambodia to enter into negotiations without any military intervention from both armies. It also signaled to Indonesia, ASEAN's chair in 2011, to be ASEAN's main representative in overseeing the retraction of troops.

Unfortunately, for many analysts, this verdict placed Thailand in a disadvantaged once more, for the provisional demilitarized zone prescribed by the ICJ not only includes the areas surrounding the temple that was the center of the ownership dispute between both countries, but also includes an area which further extends deeper into the Thai territory.

ICJ's order thus wasn't well received by the military and the foreign ministry of Thailand, intensifying the crisis.

Finally on 18 July 2012, both countries retracted their militaries from the disputed area surrounding the temple. The Association of Southeast Asian Nations (ASEAN) perceived this favorably. The 10-member ASEAN has a vested interest to mediate the conflict, partly as a signal for its own reputation and credibility. This was in line with ICJ's stance that the conflict would be better dealt with at the regional, not international, level.

However, despite these foreign interventions, and despite this primarily being a foreign policy issue, the main crux of the issue, paradoxically, still lies within the confines of Thailand's domestic politics.

Thailand's Local Politicization the Main Cause of Conflict Escalation

The resurrection of the conflict between Thailand and Cambodia mainly originated from the active politicization of this issue between various political groups. Political rivals to former Thai Prime Minister Thaksin Shinawatra, led by the yellow-shirt royalists and the Democratic Party, seized the chance to frame adversely the Preah Vihear issue so as to undermine Thanksin's proxies, accusing Thaksin of sacrificing the nations property in exchange for personal business gains in Cambodia. This subsequently sparked off one of the worst military confrontations between both countries in decades.

Back in Thailand, the protracted internal conflict has continued to serve as an impediment towards any attempts by the Yingluck government in conflict resolution and relationship building with Cambodia. The volatile relationship between her government and the military further obstructs Thai efforts.

Conflict Expands Beyond the Temple

Today, the unrelenting conflict isn't just about the sovereign rights over the Preah Vihear temple as the sole issue, but lies in the dispute of the 4.6 square kilometer area of land adjacent to the temple. Cambodia insisted the ICJ to clearly declare that the disputed area be under Cambodia's jurisdiction.

If their wishes materialize, the new ruling could spark off a sense of unhappiness and indignation among the Thais against their neighbors. This would overturn the improving bilateral ties established since under the premiership of Yingluck, Thaksin's sister.

Further Attempts at Conflict Resolution

Possibly the only silver lining among the dark clouds stems from the key bilateral cooperative frameworks reconvened under the Yngluck government. This included the 8th General Border Committee meeting held on December 19 to 20, 2011, and the 5th Joint Border Committee meeting held on February 13 to 14, 2012. Both meetings touched on issues pertaining to border demarcation and surveys of the remaining border pillars in areas beyond the Preah Vihear Temple region. However, tangible progress had been minimal.
General Neang Phat, Secretary of State of the Cambodian Defence Ministry, asserted that any delay on Thailand's part could destabilize the improved sentiments in bilateral relations between both countries.

"Cambodia has already established its Joint Working Group (JWG) and is now waiting for Thailand to set up its own JWG to deal with impending issues, such as deployment and demarcation [within the border area]." he emphasized.

He also affirmed that the tense political climate in Thailand, in which military intervention is relentless, might be the dominant obstacle challenging the progress of the JWG establishment.

A Lose-Lose Situation for Both Countries

By the middle of 2013, the ICJ will announce its reinterpretation of the scope of ownership of Cambodia's Preah Vihear Temple. It is highly possible that Cambodia might have the upper hand once more, due to the fact that Cambodia was already accorded rightful ownership of the temple way back in 1962. Other crucial factors, such as Cambodia's close working relationship with the ICJ and the United Nations since the conflict started in 2008, might further add on to Cambodia's favor.

Whichever direction the ruling materializes, it is expected that the country ruled against will not take it favorably. Unless a concerted effort are seen from both countries to recognize the legitimacy of the ICJ rulings and to prevent future militarized interventions, bitter feelings caused by this issue could remain a foreign policy risk that either country can dig up again for future confrontations.

New rounds of nationalistic sentiments could once again be stirred up, leading to more military clashes along the border. This could result in a relationship that might take several more decades to normalize.

This will in turn, further undermine the legitimacy and credibility of ASEAN as a viable platform for successful conflict resolution and security cooperation among its member states.

Foreign Policy Challenge 2

Thailand's Alliance with China versus the US: A Delicate Balance to pleasing both "Masters"

The US 'pivot' strategy towards Asia-Pacific strongly requires a reinvigoration of its security alliances with its partners in the region. In Southeast Asia, both the Philippines and Thailand have been traditional allies of the US. However, both have vastly different strategic responses and strategic options to this revitalized security engagement in the Asia-Pacific. While Manila can readily afford to adopt a more complete, embracing posture towards US military presence in the region, Bangkok can at most, adopt a "hedging strategy" with the US, with the need to keep an eye on China's show of approval on the other hand.

For Bangkok, excellent ties with Beijing provides for a better payoff, to be discussed in parts of the article. But US's ties with Thailand, coupled with Thailand's strategic engagement to US military presence, ultimately boils down to two major factors:

1) The perception of an existential threat
2) Thailand's domestic political and economic interest

The Perception of an Existential Threat

Although Thailand-US relations have long existed since 1954, Thailand has remained cautious in granting the US access to territorial assets necessary for US strategic rebalancing efforts. A striking example to this occurred when the Thai Prime Minister Yingluck Shinawatra and her government insisted in June 2011 to have the parliament first scrutinize NASA's request to use the U-tapao Airbase. Upon assertion from opposition lawmakers that the approval of NASA's request could undermine dynamic international trade relations with China, NASA withdrew the request.

This happened despite the US's long time usage of the U-tapao airbase. During the Vietnam War, the airbase has been utilized by the US to facilitate its post-disaster humanitarian efforts and military operations, most recently in the wars of Afghanistan and Iraq. Further, US troops have frequent access to the U-tapao airbase via the Cobra Gold multinational war games conducted yearly.

NASA initially intended the airbase to be used for a six-week climate study from August to September 2011. Unfortunately, due to volatile US-China relations, this proposal to use the airbase was seen as part of the 'US' pivot to Asia, and perceived as part of a wider American strategy to contain China. The Beijing government was reported as viewing NASA's request as a safeguard to US interest in Southeast Asia.

Underlying this lack of receptivity by Thailand towards US's requests for a more intimate strategic alliance stems from the lack of a common external security threat that would drive both countries to heighten their cooperation. This threat deficit has significantly affected bilateral security cooperation. Instead, while China's potential assertiveness towards Thailand might be a discerning factor in shaping the latter's foreign policy stance, Thailand nonetheless continues to push for enhanced political and economic ties with China. This phenomenal was affirmed during Yingluck's visit to Beijing in April 2011, when both countries leveled up their relations to a "comprehensive strategic cooperative partnership" status.

Another reason why Sino-Thai relations remained strong stems from the absence of any contentious territorial disputes. In contrast, US-Thai relations have been far less dynamic.

Domestic Political and Economic Interests

The value that Thailand placed with its relations with China can be traced back to its domestic economic interests. Thailand has been a great beneficiary of China's growth in the recent decade. Despite US being a major contributor of investments to Thailand, China remains the largest destination for Thailand's exports. Bilateral trade volumes between both countries amounted to US$64.7 billion in 2011, far exceeding the US$35 billion US-Thai commerce during the same year.

Figure 12: China Remains Thailand's Largest Export Destination

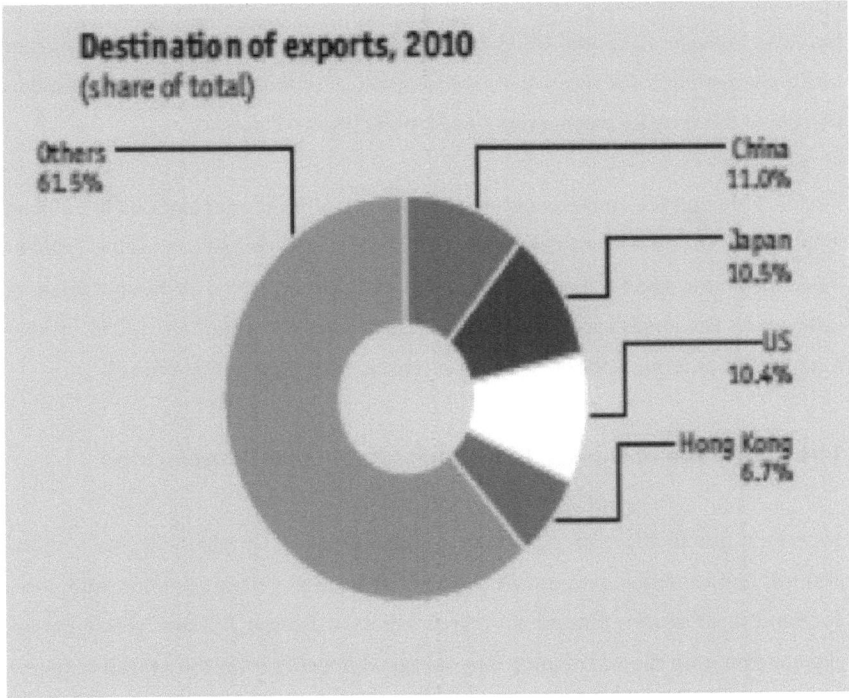

Source: McInnis CIT, EIU, EXIM, Ministry of Commerce

Additionally, as China also promised continuous assistance in Thailand's reconstruction and water conservancy projects following the disastrous floods of 2011, this effective soft power diplomacy definitely encapsulated Thailand's allegiance to China, as unsurprisingly, the latter adopted a hedging strategy.

Domestic politics constitutes the key perpetuator that contributed towards the limited progress of US-Thai bilateral collaborations. Since former Prime Minister Thaksin Shinawatra was ousted, Thailand has become more internally focused than externally. The disapproval of NASA's proposal by Bangkok only goes well to show that the country's divisive politics have much influence over security ties with Washington. Political accusations were aplenty. The opposition Democrat Party criticized Ms. Yinkluck's intention to approve NASA's request in exchange for granting Thaksin a coveted US visa. Regardless of the credibility of this criticism, one phenomenon is for sure – that intense political rivalry in the country has indeed disrupted the security partnership between the US and Thailand.

Finally, although the convergence and divergence of threat perceptions has a major role to play in influencing the outcome of US defense cooperation with Thailand, domestic political and economic concerns have taken priority over foreign relations, influencing Thailand's overall responsiveness to wards Washington's 'pivot' strategy. It appears that foreign policy is just an extension of foreign policy after all.

The Challenge of Having Limited Strategic Pre-Dispositions

Therefore, due to a lack of a common existential threat, coupled with the domestic political and economic issues, and the need to maintain close relations with China, Thailand faces severe limitations that prevents it from a full and whole-hearted engagement with the US, reaping only marginal benefits from the overall resources poured into the region by the US in support of its pivot strategy.

To illustrate this point, Thailand's engagement with the US will be contrasted with that of the Philippines, so as to serve up to readers a more distinguished contrast between the causes and effects of both varied strategic options.

A key strategic partner for the American military, Manila has adopted a more complete and embracing approach in welcoming US security policies in the region. The Manila government has granted Washington greater access to its military facilities in exchange for America's assistance in modernizing the Philippines military. And the benefits are numerous: Apart from gaining assistance from the US in the deployment of spy planes over the South China Sea, the Philippines further benefitted form the transfer of another patrol ship to the Philippine Navy, and an additional US$30 million grant in terms of military assistance.

Whether Thailand can stand to benefit more from its engagement from the US in the near future remains to be seen. As long as a lack of an existential threat persists, and as long as domestic political rivalry remains persistent, Thailand's benefit from the US might at best, remain only marginal.

Foreign Policy Challenge 3
Thailand's Indecisiveness with Regionalization

The ASEAN Community building program will materialize by 2015, in just two years time. However, despite having several Thai agencies waking up to the new regional reality and the need to act decisively to the ASEAN regionalization program, their strategy and plans that will help Thailand catch up with this development hasn't been synchronized. There is an absence of a coherent national strategy that will assist Thailand towards an effectual and material participation in the ASEAN process.

The ASEAN Community is an integration of the 10-member Association of Southeast Asian Nations (ASEAN) and their 600 million strong populations into a single community. This community is build on the fundamentals of three major pillars, namely,

1. The Political and Security Community
2. The Economic Community
3. The Social-Cultural Community

These communities are closely knitted and mutually strengthened into a cohesive whole, so as to promote enduring peace, stability and a shared prosperity in the region.

Mr. Le Luong Minh, the current ASEAN Secretary-General, is confident that ASEAN is on course to achieve the targeted date, despite this initiative being a huge undertaking. This is evident from the progress of the ASEAN Economic Community (AEC), where 259 measures or 77.54 percent of the AEC Blueprint had been successfully implemented.

Thus, how Thailand can quickly and decisively catch up with the rapid development of the ASEAN Community remains a major source of concern in the near term.

Since 2001, from the governments of Thaksin to Yingluck, Thailand has downplayed the relevance of ASEAN, preferring to focus heavily on domestic issues and administrative policies. Thaksin, especially, has paid large attentions to his overly ambitious policies, of which some of these have proven to be less than sustainable. And while Yingluck might appear committed to foreign affairs, embarking on numerous relationship-building missions globally, she has yet to have a comprehensive vision on how Thailand can fully leverage on the ASEAN Community platform. It is not too late for Yingluck to foster a coherent ASEAN strategy, given the fact that public awareness of ASEAN's relevance have heightened in recent years, but time is running out.

Additionally, the ASEAN Community isn't the only regional development that Thailand has been slow to respond to; the Trans-Pacific Partnership (TPP) has been another.

The Trans-Pacific Partnership (TPP) is the extension of the original Trans-Pacific Strategic Economic Partnership Agreement (TPSEP or P4). Initiated in 2005, the TPSEP is a free trade agreement among Brunei, Chile, New Zealand and Singapore, in an effort to create an enhanced economic liberalization of the Asia Pacific region.

But since 2010 onwards, negotiations for the TPP has taken precedence, and as of December 2012, the TPP has extended its membership to Australia, Brunei, Chile, Canada, Malaysia, Mexico, New Zealand, Singapore, Peru, the United States, and Vietnam. The TPP is purportedly intended to be a "high-standard" accord specifically targeted at emerging trade issues of the 21st century.

Notwithstanding the fact that no dateline has been allocated for countries to join the TPP cooperative framework, Thailand will still need to expedite the decision on whether it desires to be part of this cooperative. Four of its ASEAN members have already enrolled under the TPP program – Singapore, Brunei, Vietnam and Malaysia.

Perhaps, another reason for this delay boils down to the adherence of domestic bureaucratic procedures by the Thai government. Foreign Affairs Minister Surapong Towichukchaikul said, "The Thai government has to proceed according to Article 190 of the Constitution and other related processes before joining in the negotiations."

In the meantime, the Trade and Negotiation Department has already embarked on a study to determine the advantages, disadvantages and risks of finalizing the PTT agreement.

Although Thailand may have to bear the consequences of expensive medicines and other disadvantages that accompany the agreement, any further delays in the decision making process could pose additional difficulties for Thailand, mainly by stalling the country's liberalization processes. Moreover, it could allow the government a dis-inclination in improving the financial and economic facilities and systems of the country, in accordance to those in international markets.

Thailand – Facts and Figures

1. **Capital:** Bangkok
2. **Population:** 65,493,298 est. (larger than France).
3. **Language:** Thai (Siamese), Chinese, English
4. **Religion**: national religion is Buddhism (about 95% 2000 est.) followed by Muslims (about 4.5% 2000 est.)
5. **Economy world ranking**: 30th (nominal) 22nd (PPP)
6. **Currency:** Baht
7. Thailand's **total area** is about 513,120 km2 (slightly bigger than Spain)
8. Thailand is a **founding member** of the **World Trade Organization** (WTO) and of the Association of Asian Nations (**ASEAN**). ASEAN members have agreed to establish an ASEAN Free Trade Area (AFTA) by 2003. Thailand also participates in the Asia-Pacific Economic Co-operation (APEC) forum.
9. **Literacy** (age over 15 years old): Male 94.9%, Female 90.5%

Source: McInnis CMT, EIU, World Bank and Wikipedia

Outlook for 2012 – 2016

1. The victory of the Puea Thai party, led by Yingluck Shinawatra, over the Democrat Party (DP) in the July 3rd 2011 general election will not end the power struggle that has destabilized Thailand for the past five years.
2. It is only a matter of time before enmity develops between the new government and the royalist establishment, particularly if Yingluck seeks to pardon her brother, Thaksin Shinawatra, who was ousted as prime minister in 2006.
3. The Bank of Thailand (BOT, the central bank) will lower interest rates again in early 2012, but the fall in the cost of borrowing will not be on the scale seen after the 2008-09 global financial crisis.
4. Owing to severe floods, the Economist Intelligence Unit estimates that real GDP grew by just 1.2% in 2011. Growth will average 5.1% a year in the forecast period, driven largely by private consumption and investment.
5. Higher global commodity prices contributed to an acceleration of inflation in 2011, with consumer prices rising by 3.8%, but inflation will average only 3.1% a year in the forecast period.
6. Thailand's current account will remain in surplus throughout the forecast period, averaging 1.9% of GDP a year in 2012-16, buoyed by a healthy surplus on the merchandise trade account.

Source: McInnis CMT, EIU

About The Author

Dr. Tan Kwan Hong serves as professor for finance, economics, business, leadership and human resource management. Beyond his involvement as a professor, lecturer and an academic writer, he is also an award-winning corporate trainer and lecturer and has given talks to more than 120,000 people on topics such as leadership, entrepreneurship, management skills, communication skills, persuasion, career management skills and personal peak performance.

Apart from accomplishing his Doctor of Philosophy, Dr. Tan Kwan Hong has 3 Masters degrees, in particular, the Master of Science (Finance) (With Distinction) from Grenoble Ecole de Management, the Master of Science (Human Resource) (With Distinction) from Edinburgh Napier University, and the Master of Education (With High Distinction) from Monash University.

He has also obtained 3 graduate diplomas to supplement his knowledge, in particular, the Specialist Diploma in Business Analytics (With Merit) from Temasek Polytechnic, the Post Graduate Diploma in Business Administration (With High Distinction) and the Graduate Diploma in Training and Development (With High Distinction), both from Aventis School of Management in Singapore. He has scored in the top grade category for all Masters and Graduate Diploma programs, and was the overall top student for several of these programs.

Dr. Tan Kwan Hong first graduated from the Singapore Management University with the Bachelor of Science (Economics) (With Distinction).

As an avid learner, Dr. Tan Kwan Hong has also obtained more than 150 different certifications in the areas of business analytics, finance, human resource, project management and sports science. He is a Certified Business Analytics Specialist (CBAS) and a Certified Associate in Project Management (CAPM). He is also a

Distinguished Toastmasters (DTM), the highest accolade achievable from Toastmasters International, only awarded to less than 1% of all members worldwide.

As a national science champion in his youth, Dr. Tan Kwan Hong was also the recipient of several scholarships, academic and university awards, national awards, public speaking awards, and also has a national-level strategy case competition championship title. He has also represented his country in regional conferences on academic and policy issues.

Dr. Tan Kwan Hong's corporate experience spans strategy consulting, financial research, education management and policy development. He can be contacted at www.tankwanhong.com and www.linkedin.com/in/tankwanhong.